T0008767

the little book of
PALMISTRY

katalin patnaik

OH!

CONTENTS

Illustrations

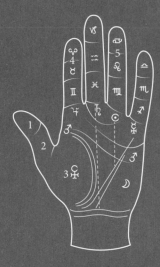

CHAPTER

1

the little book of
PALMISTRY

First published in 2023 by OH!
An Imprint of Welbeck Non-Fiction Limited,
part of Welbeck Publishing Group.
Based in London and Sydney.
www.welbeckpublishing.com

Compilation text © Welbeck Non-Fiction Limited 2022
Design © Welbeck Non-Fiction Limited 2022

Disclaimer:
This book is intended for general informational purposes only and should not be relied upon as recommending or promoting any specific practice, diet or method of treatment. It is not intended to diagnose, advise, treat or prevent any illness or condition and is not a substitute for advice from a professional practitioner of the subject matter contained in this book. You should not use the information in this book as a substitute for medication, nutritional, diet, spiritual or other treatment that is prescribed by your practitioner. The publisher makes no representations or warranties with respect to the accuracy, completeness or currency of the contents of this work, and specifically disclaim, without limitation, any implied warranties of merchantability or fitness for a particular purpose and any injury, illness, damage, death, liability or loss incurred, directly or indirectly from the use or application of any of the contents of this book. Furthermore, the publisher is not affiliated with and does not sponsor or endorse any uses of or beliefs about in any way referred in this book.

ISBN 978-1-80069-190-2

Compiled and written by: Katalin Patnaik
Editorial: Victoria Denne
Project manager: Russell Porter
Design: Andy Jones
Production: Jess Brisley

A CIP catalogue record for this book is available from the British Library

Printed in China

10 9 8 7 6 5 4 3 2 1

Illustrations: Freepik.com

INTRODUCTION and HISTORY

Palmistry, also called Chiromancy, or simply palm reading, is one of the most popular tools for divination.

You can read a person's fate, character, and get to know their skills and weaknesses, without any special tool, simply by looking at their hands!

Of course, like with all divination methods, you need to bear in mind that nothing is set in stone, and even if something is written in a person's hand, they still have the free will to change it with hard work and dedication – or the lack thereof.

Palmistry has its roots in ancient India. In fact, it is still used by Hindu priests to offer remedies to life's problems, and to advise people on important questions like marriage and business.

The use of palmistry has been historically documented from China to Egypt, as well as in ancient Greece. Palmistry likely arrived to Europe with Roma travellers, and was later adopted by occultists.

Like all other divination practices, palmistry had a bad reputation in the Middle Ages, because of the Church's view on fortune telling.

Later, during the Enlightenment, it enjoyed the interest of occultists like Casimir d'Arpentigny, William Benham and Cheiro, who revived this art and made it popular among 19th-century European practitioners.

In the 20th century, building on their predecessors' work, followers of Carl Jung reinterpreted the rules of palmistry for modern times, giving a more psychological approach to it.

There are multiple traditions of palmistry, with often contradicting interpretations for the features of the hand. It is therefore advisable to choose a version that is closest to your own heritage, and stick to that one to avoid confusion.

In this book we explore the European tradition.

There are many superstitions around palmistry, but most of them are not true in the slightest.

Reading someone's palm will not open dimensional gates for demons any more than your health practitioner checking your pulse will, for example.

Unfortunately, like with all divination practices, there are quacks who prey on curious seekers. If a palm reader tells you they can remove a deadly curse from you for a hefty amount of cash, then run!

But don't worry; most palmists are honest and knowledgeable people, who use this art to help others achieve their potential in life.

Today, palmistry enjoys great popularity among the spiritually inclined, and although the stereotype of the veiled and bejewelled palmist telling unchangeable fates is still strong in the public's mind, modern palmistry is largely about self-discovery and self-help, with an understanding of the importance of free will.

Our destiny
is in our hands – on
many levels.

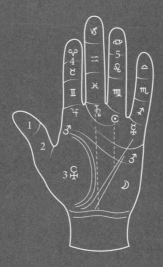

CHAPTER

2

READING
the HAND

Before you jump into interpreting the lines and mounds of the hand, it is important to take a good look at its overall appearance. Is it clean and well groomed? Is it rough and calloused, used to hard work?

You might think these observations
are part of the so-called "cold reading"
technique, but remember: you are
attempting to read a part of a person's
physical body.

Let your first impressions guide you in
forming a base image of the person, but
don't let prejudice derail
the reading.

We read the dominant hand for the practical and material status of skills, character and fate. For a right-handed person it is their right hand; for a left-handed, it is their left.

If you have an ambidextrous person, they still will have a preferred side. Asking them which hand they write with will be a good indicator.

Read that one as dominant.

The non-dominant hand shows more emotional aspects of the personality, skill set and fate the person was born with.

It is interesting to compare the two hands, to see whether there are any unutilised resources in a person's life.

Ask your seeker to show their palm, but don't give specific instructions. Observe how they extend it.

If they make their fingers straight, it means they are an open person; they are eager for you to read their palm. If their fingers are curved, they are somewhat reserved, or might feel a little anxious about the reading.

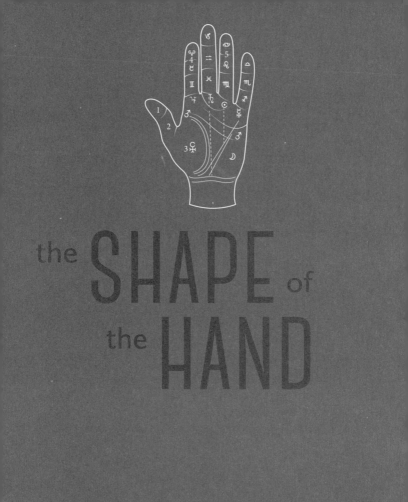

the SHAPE of the HAND

In modern palmistry, we have four types of hands, named after the four elements.

We determine this by looking at the ratio of the fingers and the palm.

the earth hand is firm, and it has a square palm and short fingers. This person is dependable, helpful, steadfast and honest.

They are creative and enjoy doing things with their hands, be it gardening, sculpting or baking.

They do well at professions where attention to detail and being grounded are key.

the fire hand is flexible and warm, and it has a long palm and short fingers.

This person is very active, competitive and spontaneous. They usually love sports. They are natural leaders, and enjoy being in the spotlight.

They do well in performing arts and leadership roles.

the air hand is is soft and dry,
and it has a square palm and long
fingers.

This person is intelligent, diplomatic
and logical. They enjoy mental
stimulation, and are great at
communicating their opinions and
ideas. They are also good at time
management.

They do well in professions that require
intellectual creativity.

the water hand is soft and moist, and both the palm and the fingers are long.

This person is emotional, empathetic and spiritual. They are excellent at reading people, they have a vivid imagination, and are very intuitive. They might have special gifts like clairvoyance, and an affinity to spiritual practices.

They do well in professions that require empathy.

THE FLEXIBILITY OF THE HAND

The more flexible the hand is, the more flexible the person.

If the fingers can be bent backwards, it means the person has a unique point of view; they are able to see things differently than others. They enjoy life, and are ready for whatever comes next.

Stiff fingers that don't bend backwards suggest a more orthodox, traditional person who has a set of values they keep themselves to.

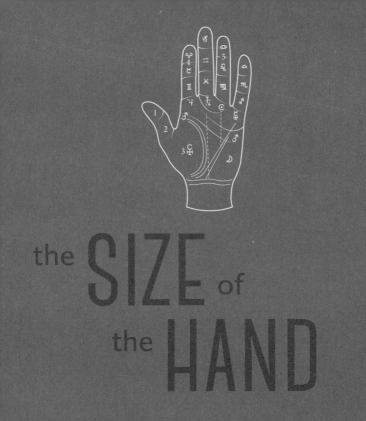

the SIZE of
the HAND

Whatever the shape of the hand is, its size gives us valuable clues, too.

A large hand amplifies the meaning of the hand's shape, while a small hand reduces its effect on the personality.

A large hand means the person has a great eye for detail.

They are hard to cheat, as they catch the smallest inconsistencies.

A small hand indicates a flamboyant, open-minded person.

They are often artistic, sometimes a bit erratic and disorderly in how they deal with everyday tasks.

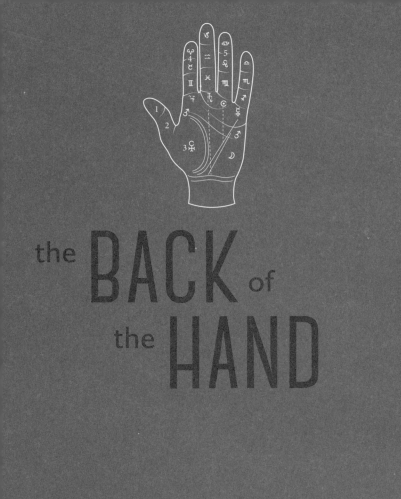

the BACK of
the HAND

This can reveal how we deal with life's challenges. The softer the skin, the smoother the person's lifestyle is, while coarse, rough skin indicates a tougher person who swims against the tide.

HAIR ON THE HAND

The hair on the hand indicates a person's physicality and vitality.

The stronger, coarser the hair is, the stronger the person physically, while fine hair indicates a delicate frame.

Thick hair on the hand indicates a creative person full of ideas, while a thin hair shows a person with fewer, but more refined ideas.

Hair on all fingers shows a
hardworking person who doesn't
like wasting their time.

Hair on the thumb shows a highly
creative, imaginative person.

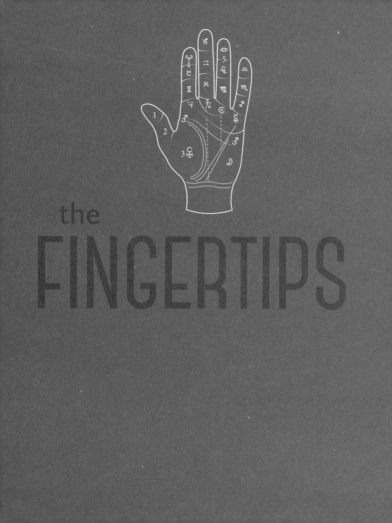

the
FINGERTIPS

The shapes of the fingertips
provide an additional nuance to
the basic picture you have built
so far.

There are four shapes, and it is possible that each finger has a different one, in which case the person's nature is very complex.

If there is a dominant shape, that defines the person's character more than any other shape found on their fingers.

A finger is **conic** if the tip has
   a gentle arch. This indicates
   impulsiveness and intuitiveness.

A finger is **pointed** if the tip narrows sharply. This indicates creativity and sensitivity.

A finger is **square** if it stays level to the end, and has a flat tip. This indicates practicality and traditionalism.

A finger is **spatulate** if it gets wider at the tip. This indicates lots of energy and enthusiasm.

Combine these meanings with those of each specific finger to get a more detailed reading.

GAPS BETWEEN THE FINGERS

Ask the person to keep their hand on the table, and relax.

If there are gaps between their fingers, it means they are individualistic; they follow their heart in life.

If their fingers stay close to each other, they are traditionalists who like rules and laws. They are no-nonsense people.

THE POSITIONING
OF THE FINGERS

How straight a line the fingers form on the hand indicates how successful a person can become.

A straight line shows the potential of success in whatever the person wants to achieve.

Arched fingers, where the index
and little fingers form an arch, show
struggles in life and diminished
strength of the low-sitting fingers.

KNUCKLES

The size of the knuckles shows how prudent or whimsical the person is. Ask the person to lay their hand fingers straight, palm down on the table.

If they have well visible, protruding knuckles, they are careful and sensible people. If their knuckles are smooth and flat, they are whimsical and artistic.

THE JOINTS

Smooth joints indicate a person who listens to their feelings about situations and people, while knotty joints show a person who uses their head more than their heart.

DROPLETS

Droplets are little bumps on the top pads that look like a waterdrop hanging on the finger. You can see these better by turning the hand palm down, and relaxing the fingers.

If they are present, then the person is very sensitive; they could even be empaths or psychics. If there are no droplets, the person is very down to earth and logically minded.

THE NAILS

Look at the nails of the person.

The longer they are, the more imaginative the person is; the shorter the nails, the more pragmatic the person. Narrow nails show narrowmindedness, while wide nails indicate an open-minded person.

Check the nails for moons –
crescent-shaped white sections
at the bases of nails. Small moons
indicate good health, but large
ones suggest the possibility of
health problems.

If there are no moons, the person's
health could easily be affected by
their circumstances and their state
of mind.

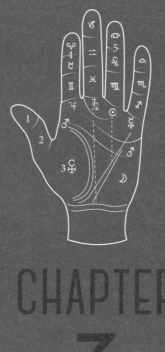

CHAPTER

3

the FINGERS

The fingers are named after
Roman gods, except for the thumb,
which doesn't have a special
name. Knowing mythology helps
to remember the meanings of the
fingers, but it isn't essential; in this
section, we will explore the
fingers in detail.

the THUMB

The thumb shows a
person's temper, and their
strength of mind.

A normal thumb is about the same length as the little finger, and when held next to the palm, it reaches halfway up the first section of the index finger.

A person with a normal thumb is good at team work. They can take charge of a situation if needed, they have healthy boundaries, and they can take constructive criticism well.

A person with a long thumb can be bossy. They like to be in charge at all times. They don't take criticism well. An extremely long thumb could indicate a bully.

A short thumb means an easy-going person who likes to go with the flow. They don't feel comfortable in leadership roles, and are good at taking orders from others.

The thumb is divided into two phalanges, or sections. The top phalange shows the person's willpower. The longer this section is, the more determined the person. The thicker this phalange, the greater lengths the person is prepared to go to to get what they want.

The middle phalange of the thumb shows decision-making, and how a person handles different situations. A long middle phalange indicates someone who doesn't rush into decisions.

A short middle section indicates the opposite: this person thinks well on their feet. A thin middle phalange shows a diplomatic person who easily finds the common tone with others.

The position of the thumb on the palm shows the person's level of ego. A normal thumb's middle phalange starts around the middle of the palm.

The higher up it is towards the index finger, the greater the person's ego is, while a low-sitting thumb shows lesser ego.

The angle of the thumb with the palm shows how outgoing someone is. A normal angle is between 45 and 90 degrees, which means the person is open and confident, and has healthy boundaries.

If it is smaller than 45 degrees, then it is a very reserved, cautious person. If the angle is bigger than 95 degrees, they are very open, have few boundaries, and spend their money and energy freely – maybe overly so.

the JUPITER or INDEX finger

The Jupiter finger shows a person's pride, and their relationship with power.

A normal Jupiter finger reaches up
to the half of the middle finger's
last phalange.

It shows a person who takes pride
in their achievements, but doesn't
become haughty when success
finds them.

A long Jupiter finger shows a person who is prone to become arrogant. They are ambitious, and might crave power over others. To see how they handle power, look at their thumb.

A short Jupiter finger shows a good helper. They don't crave power or fame; they are happy being there for others. They are good at following orders.

Ask the seeker to hold their fingers
straight together, and look out for
gaps between them. If there is a
gap between the Jupiter and Saturn
(middle) finger, this person is great
at managing time and resources.

the SATURN
or MIDDLE
finger

The Saturn finger shows a
person's sense of duty.

A normal Saturn finger is around three quarters of the palm's length.

A person with a normal length Saturn finger has a good sense of work–life balance.

A person with a long Saturn finger often feels bound to take on more and more responsibilities, even though they might have enough on their plate already.

A person with a short Saturn finger isn't good with commitments, be it in relationships or at work.

If there is a gap between the Saturn
and the Apollo (ring) finger, the
person lives in the moment.

the APOLLO or RING finger

The Apollo finger shows
a person's creativity and
emotional maturity.

A normal Apollo finger is slightly shorter than the Jupiter finger.

A person with a normal Apollo finger has well-regulated emotions, and doesn't have a problem with expressing them. They appreciate arts, whether they actually partake in creating or not.

A person with a long Apollo finger is highly emotional, and very artistic.

A person with a short Apollo finger has a practical mindset, and might not appreciate fine arts. Functionality takes priority over form in their book. They may find it hard to express their emotions.

A gap between the Apollo and
Mercury (little) finger shows a
person who often has their head in
the clouds.

the
MERCURY
or LITTLE
finger

The Mercury finger shows a
person's communication skills.

A normal Mercury finger reaches the bottom of the top phalange of the Apollo finger.

When measuring this finger, take care to bring the two fingers to the same level, because the Mercury finger often sits lower on the palm, and looks shorter than it actually is.

A person with a normal Mercury finger has a good ability to express themselves, but they are likely not very exuberant with their words.

A person with a long Mercury finger
finds it easy to express themselves
with innovative and flowery
phrases. They are masters of their
language, and are very entertaining.

A person with a short Mercury
finger may find it difficult to
communicate with others, and to
put their thoughts into words.

Check the shape of the finger.
If it is straight, the person is
trustworthy. If the Mercury finger is
crooked, they are less so.

CHAPTER

4

the LINES

Our palms are riddled with lines.
They differ from person to person,
and even from hand to hand on the
same person.

The strength of the line defines the strength of the area in your life that it is associated with.

A line is considered weak if it is faint, or it isn't one continuous line, but consists of tiny "feathers", it has boxes or bubbles in it, or if it has other, small lines crossing it.

If any lines are missing, that means the person doesn't fully embrace that energy in their lives.

The start of each line shows a person's childhood, while the end shows the person's last days.

The direction of each line will be important for predictions and timing.

NOTE:

When describing the position of
some lines in this chapter I will
often refer to the Mounts. These
are discussed in Chapter 5, but a
clear diagram of all the Mounts can
be found on pages 160-161.

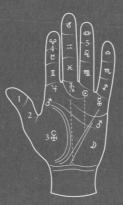

the LIFE LINE

The Life line shows a person's
health and energy levels.
It starts between the thumb
and the Jupiter finger, and curls
around the pad under the thumb.

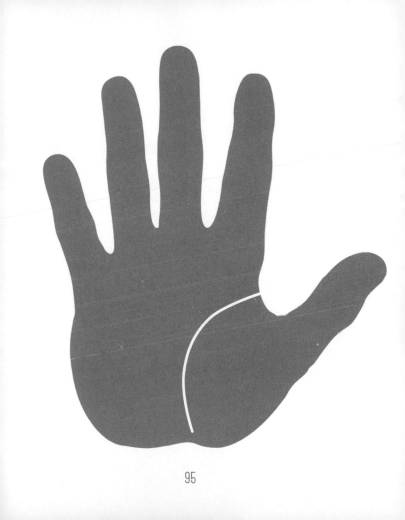

95

A normal Life line starts midway between the thumb and the Jupiter finger, and denotes a person who knows their mind, but are not overly ambitious.

A Life line that starts near the Jupiter finger shows a person who is very ambitious and determined.

A Life line that starts near the thumb shows a person who is not ambitious, and likes to spend more time with their loved ones or their hobbies than on their career.

A Life line that has a weak start shows a troubled childhood, while a weak line at the end shows the person's energy will slowly dissipate towards the end.

This doesn't necessarily mean an illness, so do not make a prognosis.

The gap between the Head line (see page 112) and the Life line shows how well this person can make their own decisions.

A fused Head and Life line shows an indecisive, dependant person, while a person with a big gap between the two is highly independent.

The length of the Life line does not correspond to the length of a person's life.

Someone with a short, but strong Life line may live to a hundred years.

The curve of the line shows
the person's level of joie de vivre
– how much they are capable of
enjoying life.

The more curved the line, the more
carefree and giving the person is,
while a straight line shows a very
serious, possibly selfish person.

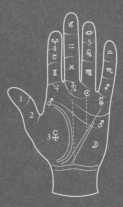

the # HEART LINE

The Heart line shows a person's emotional intelligence, and stance to love. It starts under the Mercury finger, and could end anywhere under the Saturn or Jupiter fingers.

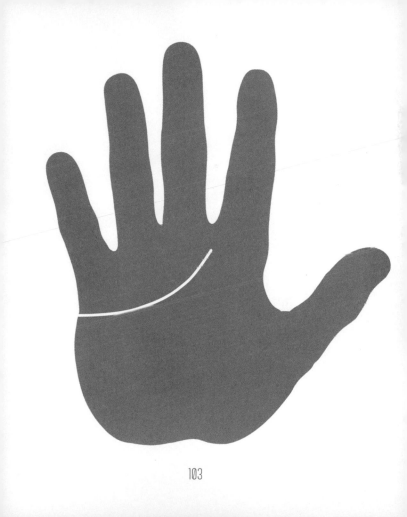

103

A strong Heart line shows a person who is steady and loyal, and who finds it easy to commit, be it to people or to projects.

A weak Heart line shows someone
who needs constant stimulation.
They get bored easily, and
are always on the lookout for
adventures and new projects.

The length of the line tells you
about how secure the person is in
their relationships.

A long Heart line that goes across the whole palm shows an emotionally needy person. They want their partner to forget about the rest of the world, and be exclusively theirs. They can be quite jealous and demanding.

A Heart line that ends under the
Jupiter finger shows a person who
is loyal and has deep emotions
towards their loved ones – friends,
family and partners.

A Heart line ending between the Jupiter and Saturn fingers shows a person who combines the characteristics of both fingers. They are loyal and sensual, and realistic.

A Heart line ending under the Saturn finger shows a person who gives great importance to their emotional life.

They are very sensual, which sometimes overrides their better judgement. They might cheat on their partners, and they find it hard to learn from their mistakes.

The curve of the Heart line tells us
about the person's empathy levels.
The more curved it is, the more
empathetic the person, while if it
is a straight line, they can come
across as unfeeling.

The position of the Heart line tells us how openly a person shows their affection.

The normal position of the Heart line is in the middle between the fingers and the Head line. The higher the line, the easier the person finds it to show signs of affection. The closer to the Head line it is, the more introverted the person. It doesn't mean they aren't capable of love; they may feel deeply, but they find it hard to show it.

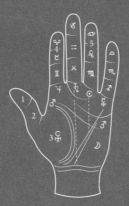

the HEAD LINE

The Head line shows a person's intellectual abilities, their thought process. It starts near the thumb, and runs more or less parallel to the Heart line.

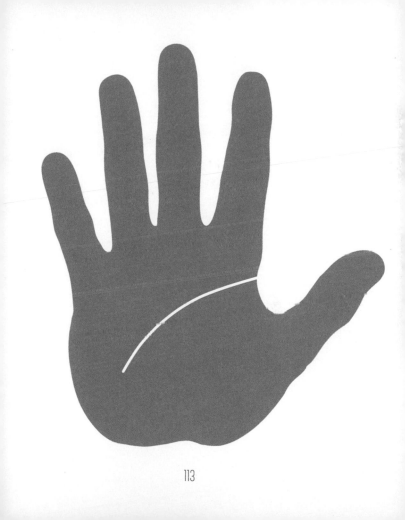

The position of the Head line tells us about a person's confidence in their mental capability. The nearer to the Jupiter finger it starts, the more self-assured the person is, the easier they make decisions and take risks.

If it starts near the thumb, the person lacks self-confidence, and can be overly cautious and quiet in social situations.

The length of the Head line shows a person's decision-making process.

The shorter it is, the quicker the person makes their decisions, while a long Head line that ends near the edge of the palm means the person likes to mull over problems and choices.

The shape of the Head line shows
the way the person thinks.

A straight line means the person
is a logical thinker; they have a
common-sense approach to life
with little imagination.

If the Head line is curved, has a
slope, or is not straight in any
way, that means the person has a
good imagination, and can be very
inventive.

If the Head line ends in a fork, the person is able to see both sides of an argument, and is able to remain impartial and objective in most situations.

If the Head line curves up towards a finger, that finger's energy will rule the person's thought process.

The distance between the Head and Heart lines tells us about how open-minded the person is.

The closer the two lines are, the more reserved and traditionalist the person is, while if there is a big gap between them, the person is open-minded and quite liberal.

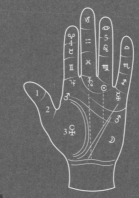

the
SIMIAN LINE

If the Head line and the Heart
line are fused together, it is called
the Simian line.

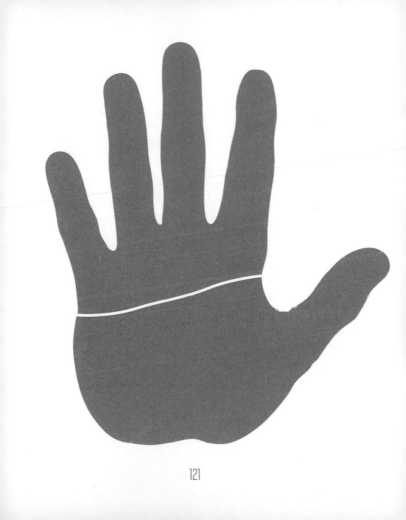

121

The Simian line starts between the
thumb and the Jupiter finger, and
ends near the edge of the palm,
between where the Head and Heart
lines would normally be.

It is very rare to see a Simian
line, and their owners are equally
remarkable.

People with a Simian line don't differentiate between emotions and thoughts. They feel deeply and are very intense in their actions and emotions.

They may have trouble establishing a work–life balance, especially with romantic partners. They are driven and determined, and often get what they want.

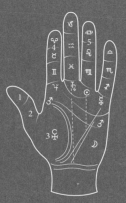

the FATE LINE

The Fate line shows the person's drive, career, and the direction of their life. It starts at the base of the palm, and goes horizontally towards the fingers.

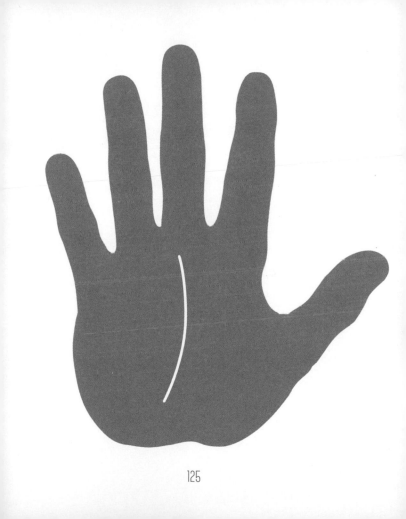

125

There are three places the
Fate line can start: on the Mount
of the Moon, on the Mount of
Venus, and between the two (see
Chapter 5).

If the line starts on the Mount of
the Moon, the person is headstrong
and individualistic. They burn
out easily, so they need constant
stimulation.

If the Fate line starts on the Mount of Venus, the person honours their family's expectations and wishes above their own. They can become quite orthodox in their thinking.

If the Fate line starts between the two mounts, the person will find a good balance between his own and his family's wishes, and will be able to strike a deal that suits everyone.

The altitude of the line tells us how soon a person finds their calling.

A line that starts near the wrist shows a person who always knew what they wanted to be, while if it starts higher up on the palm, it means they found themselves later on.

A Fate line is considered normal if it ends at the Heart line.

In this case, the person will stop working at retirement age, and will have no more interest in the job they used to do before.

A short Fate line ends at the Head
line, and means that the person will
lose interest in their career, and
may even lose direction in their life.
It is a possible sign of a complete
burnout.

A long fate line that ends above the Heart line means the person will stay involved with their interests even after retirement, for the rest of their life.

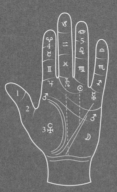

the MINOR LINES

1. the line of mars
2. the line of apollo
3. the line of mercury
4. the lines of marriage
5. the lines of children
6. the girdle of venus
7. the bracelets of neptune
8. the ring of solomon
9. the medical stigmata
10. the line of neptune
11. the line of ranus
12. travel lines
13. influence lines
14. support lines
15. worry lines

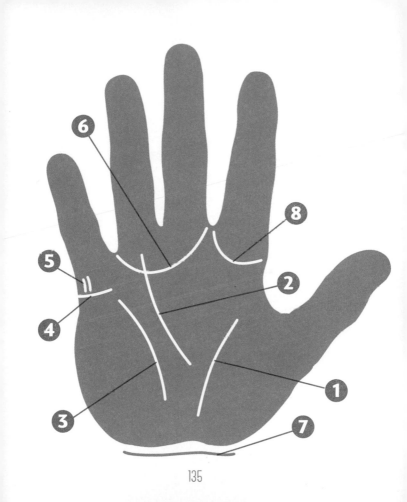

135

the line of mars starts below the Life line, and ends on the Mount of Venus.

It means the person has good energy levels, and has a special talent – for a clue as to what this might be, look at other marks on the palm.

❷

the line of apollo can start
anywhere around the middle of the
palm, and ends on the Mount of Apollo.
It shows a person's way to success and
satisfaction, in some cases to fame. If it
starts at the base of the palm, it means
the person will be very successful thanks
to their hard work. If the line starts
around the Life line, it means they will be
supported in their quest to success. If it
starts around the Head line, the person is
very determined to get what they want,
and they often do. If the line starts near
the Heart line, then the person's goals
are very close to their heart, and they will
pour a lot of energy into achieving them.

the line of mercury starts at
the base of the palm and goes upwards
to the Mount of Mercury.

Not having this line is good news,
because it indicates problems with
health. If it is present, the weaker it is,
the more care the person has to take
with their health and mental wellbeing.
An extremely weak line might indicate
a hypochondriac.

4

the lines of marriage are situated on the side of the hand, under the Mercury finger and above the Heart line. They show the number of romantic relationships that leave a high impact on the person, be it marriage or a long-term relationship.

5

the lines of children are

vertical lines situated between the Mercury finger and the top marriage line. They show the number of potential pregnancies.

A strong line shows a healthy child, while a weak line can show potential problems during the pregnancy. Again, avoid giving a prognosis.

6

the girdle of venus runs

more or less parallel to the Heart line.
It can start anywhere between the
Jupiter and Saturn fingers, and ends
on the Mount of Apollo or Mercury.
It shows to what extent a person's
mood affects their actions, and how
passionate they are in general.

A strong Girdle of Venus indicates a
highly passionate, capricious person,
while someone with a weak or missing
line has a better control of their
impulses.

7

the bracelets of neptune

are the circular lines around the wrist. They are easier to see if you bend the hand. A normal hand has two bracelets. They show a person's health and luck in life.

The more bracelets a person has, the luckier they are, while the quality of the bracelets indicates their level of health. The bracelet nearest to the palm dominates the interpretation.

the ring of solomon is a

circular line on the Mount of Jupiter
that looks like a ring under the finger. It
indicates strong empathetic, and often
psychic, abilities.

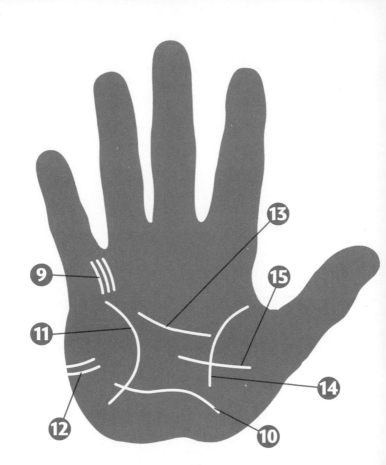

the medical stigmata are a
group of short, parallel lines situated on
the Mount of Mercury.

It indicates that a person's compassion
levels are very high. They feel called
to help others, be it professionally,
through donation to good causes, or
as a friend who is always there in
difficult times.

⑩

line of Neptune, or via lascivia,
starts under the thumb, near the end
of the life line, and runs across the
hand towards the Mount of the Moon.

It shows the person could easily get
addicted to alcohol, cigarette, drugs,
or even to sex. They need to be
very careful, and keep their "guilty
pleasures" in check.

⑪

line of uranus is a semicircle
that starts on the Mount of the Moon,
touches the middle of the palm, and
ends on the Mount of Mercury. It
shows a person with great talent for
the psychic arts.

If it is broken, it could mean these
talents are affecting the person
negatively, like an empath continuously
overwhelmed by the feelings they pick
up from others. It is worth attending
proper training in whatever field of the
occult the person chooses to explore.

travel lines run on the side of the palm, starting below the head line. The more lines there are, the more time the person will spend travelling.

Upwards curling travel lines indicate good outcomes, while downwards curling ones foretell unsuccessful trips.

influence lines are small lines
running horizontally across the palm.
They show that other people have
great influence on the person.

14

support lines are lines that run next to any other line, so it looks like the person has, for example, two Life lines. These lines strengthen the energy of the ones they support.

worry lines are small lines in any direction on the palm. They show the person worries a lot about what others think.

OTHER

MARKS

crosses mean problems and obstacles in the area of life their position shows, except the Crosses of Mystics.

the crosses of mystics

(la croix mystique) are crosses
between the Head and Heart
lines. They show a talent for
occult practices and spirituality.

stars are similar to crosses, but have more arms. A star has at least five arms. They denote great difficulties at the area of life they appear on.

triangles are formed by major and minor lines crossing each other – for example by the Fate, the Head and the Mercury lines.

Do not count small, faint triangles that might appear. They show that education and training is important to the person; they are highly likely to go to college, and enjoy learning new skills throughout their lives.

the letter M formed by the Major lines on the palm shows a very lucky person with strong intuition and determination.

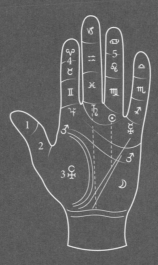

CHAPTER

5

the MOUNTS

The mounts are the padded parts of the palm under the fingers and the thumb. They are indicative of the person's energy level in the mount's associated area of life.

the MOUNTS

1. the mount of jupiter
2. the mount of saturn
3. the mount of apollo
4. the mount of mercury
5. the outer mount of mars
6. the mount of the moon
7. the mount of venus
8. the inner mount of mars
9. the plain of mars

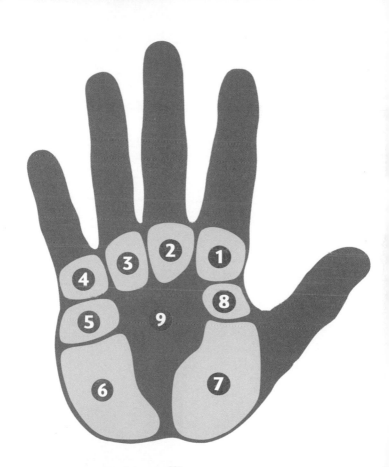

the mount of jupiter

is placed under the Jupiter finger, and
it shows a person's leadership qualities
and ambitiousness.

The fleshier the mount is, the bossier the person.

An extremely fleshy Mount of Jupiter shows a dictator type of personality, especially if the Jupiter finger and the thumb are also prominent, while a flat or missing mount indicates a person who likes to go with the flow, and has little to no ambition.

2

the mount of saturn

is placed under the Saturn finger, and it shows how responsible and disciplined a person is.

The fleshier the mount is, the more hardworking and dutiful the person. An extremely fleshy Mount of Saturn shows a person who is prone to taking on all the responsibilities by themselves, be it at work or in their family. They can become bitter and resentful, often feeling like a martyr.

A thin mount of Saturn shows a person who doesn't really care about duties and responsibilities, and likes others to take care of them.

A merged Jupiter and Saturn Mount shows a person who is very ambitious and resourceful, and therefore is very capable of attaining their goals.

③

the mount of apollo

is placed under the Apollo finger, and shows the person's level of creativity and sociableness, and their appreciation for fine things.

The fleshier the mount is, the more eccentric the person. An extremely fleshy mount shows a highly creative person who might be a bit of a show-off, while a flat mount shows a conformist who doesn't really care for arts.

A merged Saturn and Apollo Mount
shows the mindset of a professional
artist: they are creative, and they can
make a living out of their creative
passion.

the mount of mercury

is placed under the Mercury finger, and shows a person's level of expertise in communication.

The fleshier the mount is, the better communicator the person.

An extremely fleshy Mount of Mercury
shows an eloquent and diplomatic
person, who knows how and what to
tell whom, while a flat mount shows
someone who finds it hard to put their
thoughts and feelings into words.

A merged Apollo and Mercury Mount shows a person whose creativity manifests in communication, like an author, a DJ, or a marketing manager.

the outer mount of mars

is placed directly under the Mount of Mercury, and above the Mount of the Moon. It shows a person's level of integrity.

An extremely fleshy Outer Mount of Mars indicates a person with extremely strong beliefs, to the point of narrow-minded dogmatism.

A flat mount shows a person who is easily swayed in any direction.

the mount of the moon
is the fleshy part under the Outer
Mount of Mars. It shows the person's
intuition and level of empathy.

The fleshier the mount is, the more intuitive and imaginative the person.

An extremely fleshy mount shows someone with a vivid imagination that they might confuse with reality, while a flat mount shows a person who stands with both feet on the grounds of reality, and has no care for flights of fancy.

A low-sitting Mount of the Moon that
ends under the Mount of Venus shows
a highly intuitive, highly perceptive
person. They might even be psychic.

A high-sitting mount shows a
person who might find it difficult to
understand other people's feelings.

the mount of venus

is the pad that connects the thumb
to the base of the palm. It shows the
person's general health, and how they
express themselves.

The fleshier the mount is, the healthier
the person.

An extremely fleshy mount shows a
person who is very healthy with high
energy levels, and who might have
a high sex drive, while a flat mount
shows a person who might be prone
to sickness and may find it difficult to
warm up to others.

8

the inner mount of mars

is placed directly under the Mount of Jupiter, and above the Mount of Venus. It shows a person's level of courage and bravery.

An extremely fleshy Inner Mount of Mars indicates a foolhardy person who jumps into action without first thinking things through. A flat mount means a person who can come across as cowardly and avoids conflicts if they can.

9

the plain of mars

is the centre of the palm, enclosed
by all the mounts. It shows a person's
morale and self-assuredness.

Because the Plain of Mars is not a mount that is visually assessable, we determine the quality of the plain by touch.

A normal plain is firm and elastic.
A thick and hard plain shows a person
who is overconfident and can be
inconsiderate in their actions, while
a thin, bony Plain of Mars shows a
diffident person who takes great pains
in avoiding conflict and risks in general.

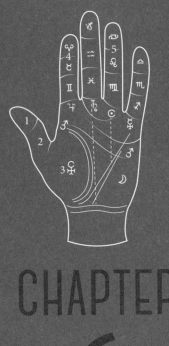

CHAPTER

READING
the PALM

It is a good idea to establish a sequence to your reading that you follow every time, to avoid missing any clues.

Make a list of marks and features that support each other. If one feature is weak, check the status of all the others. Always consider the whole of the hand.

Practice on your own palm first,
because it will be easy to relate the
lines and their meanings to your
own life.

It can be interesting to analyse famous people's photos where their hands are at least partially visible.

For example, Grigori Rasputin had a very fleshy Mount of Venus, showing that the rumours of his sexual appetite were likely true. Look up a picture of your favourite actor's hands: how does it relate to their public persona?

When reading for others, always
ask for permission before touching
their hands. You don't want to
startle them by grabbing their hand
to massage their Plain of Mars!

Sometimes a magnifying glass
and a strong light source might
be needed to be able to see the
markings clearly.

If you see an indicator of bad health, remain gentle and tactful.

Never make a medical diagnosis.

Instead, advise the person to pay attention to their health.

When making predictions, imagine the lines representing the average life span of 75 years.

Divide the lines to equal portions, each portion representing approximately ten years.

Remember, every line has a
fixed starting point that represents
childhood; start your calculation
there.

Fully learning to
read a hand will take
practice.

Be patient with
yourself, and you will
get there.